HIDE & SEEK

Self-explanatory

1993-1998

Robert E. Rose

This is the start of a collection sires of several books to come

Book. I.	Self-explanatory	1993-1998
Book. II.	How & what am I to thrust & believe	1993-1998
Book. III.	Moonstruck	1997-2002
Book. IV.	A hypothetical, illogical situation	1989-2004
Book. V.	Another book of words	1993-2003

These are the first five in the collection

All written between 1989-2004 by: Robert E. Rose
Except, *If written by: Robert E. Rose & Casper Hyde

Tropical Storm Writings

ISBN 978-8-7711-4120-7

THANX

Everything in theses books
are all written by me and there by are a part of me
showcasing what's going on in my mind.
Yes most of it is free imagination
but some of it are also part memories, dreams,
reality and fiction

I hope people see this as an attempt to adapt
all of that on to paper,
but in a way that each individual in there own way
may have a separate understanding or a lack of.

They are all mostly dark and one mite
find it hard to see anything positive in them
but there is. And there is some humor, love,
weirdness and seriousness in them too.

Keep reading, keep thinking,.

HIDE & SEEK
Self-explanatory 1993-1998

1.	-UFO- (so this is it) ?!... part. 1.	1997
2.	Equipment	1996
3.*	If.	'93&'95
4.	Always complaining & * ?	1995
5.	- Bewildered -	1997
6.	Created a riot	1997
7.	Bird's of trust. Part. 1.	1997
8.	Subsequently	1996
9.	If we stumble, this is why	1996
10.	Absent.	1996
11.	-UFO- (so this is it) ?!... part. 2.	1997
12.	Bird's of trust. Part. 2.	1997
13.	Cooperation	1996
14.	You & me	1994
15.	- Jailcity'96 -	1996
16.	…..but can't…..	1996
17.	-UFO- (so this is it) ?!... part. 3.	1997
18.	<u>- A redwood forest -</u>	1995
19.	Occasionally requiring maintenance	1996
20.	Ongoing & oncoming	1996
21.	Extravagant wall of flames	'95&'96
22.	Flood.	1996
23.	Coo coo !	1996
24.	10 stoies up - part 2 of 2 out of 15.	1997
25.	From the sky. Part. 1.	1998
26.	- A beach bitch bench -	1997
27.	Another ordinary day	1996
28.	Manipulation.	1997
29.	Out. Part. 1.	1994
30.	Think.	1997

By : Robert E. Rose
Except * by : Casper Hyde & Robert E. Rose

-UFO- (so this is it) ?!… part. 1.

You don't know what's going on.

& you're standing in the wind
As I'm flying by in a blue -UFO-

& you're twisting & turning in the wind
With an empty look on your face
& now you're gone'

So is this it…So this is it.

EQUIPMENT

How long must I wait
Before I can go, go away
Go on with my life.

It's too late
It's all just a mistake.

I have no weapons
              So why run away from me in fear
I haven't got any equipment
              So why come to me for help

How long must I wait
Before you can see, see the sea
See which way to go

It's a dead-end
It's all just too much for me

I have no answers
              So why ask me what to do
I haven't got any equipment
              So why look at me in that way

How long can I, must I wait
        How long, how long.

RER'96 21/6

IF.

The blind children all play in the streets of plag
Birds fly heavily beneath the sultry sun not frightened by the old gun

What would our women say
If we had no love for them to stay

What would our children think
If they had no water to drink

A lost man roams around in the remains of what's left
Fish swim highly above the dying bottom not thinking of the atom bomb

What would our people say
If we had no food to feed us with

What would our world do
If we began to be the only thing left

What would our soul's do
If they had no resting place

Where would we go,… if we could ?.

Casper & Robert '93&'95   RER'95 29/1

Always complaining. &*?

In a desert somewhere
Running throw the sand somehow

All this uncultivated land
Now covered by the snow

Al these enormous areas
Now stripped of all hope

How can the clouds hang
So low over the masses

In a place with open spaces
Digging throw the unharmed ground

All this and now only so little left

All these numerous art's out here
KILL'D by US as we still stand
And fight with each other

How can I alter your point of view
When you never say a thing to me

How can the shout's last so long
In the thickening sky above

I could never quite find you----------in playing water

I could never quite see you----------in dancing dust

And now it's too much.

BEWILDERED

On a beach…..stranded
Lost…..in an unknown place

How could this in anyway be real

Bewildered
Trapped within my self
Fighting with my self

Running away from the sunset
                For to greet it a-little sooner
                Oh to meet it on the other side
                Just to see which of us could get there first   (who do you think won)

You stole my trust
You took my love
You used me
You took it all…& know….. You sing like I…..in vain
        & know…..you stand like me…..in shame

Feel like a bird flying freeee…. . . . . . .ly
        Flying FAST
        Flying f a r
        Flying finely

Stop the train, I'm getting off
        I'm feeling sick & out of control

Stop the plane, I'm getting out
        I'm feeling slick & out of order

Let's go…go away…away from here
Let's go…go out…out side & play
Let's go…go on…on with what we do'!?………

On a beach…..lost
Stranded…..in a place unknown

How can this ever be real
How can this ever be enough
How could there ever in anyway not be more …..than this.

RER'97 14/10

Birds of trust / part. 1.

                        Bird of trust fly's out the window

                        Bird of lust flying out in to the open

                                         & now it's back in it's cage
                                         & someone's happy I guess

                        Bird of lust flying out into the enclosement

                        Bird of trust fly's without wisdom

Subsequently

Can't believe it's become this way
Can't believe in anything

I don't know if you can   understand
Why everything's so   complicated

I can't support my self
Can't correct my self
Can't even help my self

Needing to know what's going on outside
As your bleeding inside
Leaving us all to die

Why is everything so   complicated
I don't think you   understand

I can't see the tree's from all the burning wood
Can't hear the bird's from all the nearby shooting
Can't even find my self

Can't believe it's come to this
Can't believe in what I see
Can't believe it's subsequently coming to an end

Can't believe it's all so unbelievable

If we stumble, this is why

So this is the beginning of an end
   We have become unaware
        Of what we do'

& this is why
We all fall apart
Deep inside of our self's

        It's too much for us
        Our past & root's

   & if we stumble now
  It's because we all start to slowly
Loose grasp of reality

So this is why
We all stay away
Far from our own feelings

        & so yes we've come far
        In many ways
        But still there is so much more to see, learn - to do, & experience

Oh the pace is to fast for us
But we've got to keep up or else we'll stumble

& this is why, oh this is why
I can't let <u>go</u>, no can't say <u>no</u>

ABSENT

      So I keep my thoughts
           All to my self

    I know it's unhealthy

    & pick's & tares at one
        Until you feel twisted
              & all curled-up in & out
                  Side

Outside
It's not today
    I thought it was
        But wrong again

    Disappointed & unanswered
        Me & my questions

I don't think
    I'll ever really know

So I'm a man
& it seams like you expect
        Me to know everything

                But am I not just
                A man of the world

                Trying to pull all the pieces
                Together

Apparently mistaken
    & out of the sky
      I see it all
    See it all fall

    & now I'm lost
        Cause I couldn't move

& I didn't know why
    I didn't care
        Wasn't really sure,   until now

RER'96 28/11

-UFO- (so this is it) ?!... part. 2.

You don't know what's going on

& you're standing in the way
As I try to land my blue -UFO-

I see you crushed & flattened by the weight
With a misplaced expression on your face
& now you're dead'

So is it this…..so this it is

Birds of trust / part. 2.

Birds flying south for the winter

Birds flying north for the summer

An eagle in pain
A swan in vain

& I'm looking up at a flock of swallows

A seagull in-sane
An owl in the rain

Birds flying west for the fun of it

Birds flying east for the experience

- COOPERATION -

This complex structure resembles
    Microscopic molecules in need of aid

      Committed to an endless journey
          Haunted by my own realization

Scientific pharmaceuticals take action
      This is an improvement yea'

            I
         Experienced
            A
         Discussion
            Of
         Pleasure

      As uncomfortably as I am
    The population prevents the expectancy

Quiet hostility
    Quality affirmative
        Quick cooperation
                            & immigration has an optimistic innovation of
                                    Advancement

          Hurry
              It's
                  Coming

      Money laundering research

                    & unanswered words
            Gives me the urge
        To go on…. .   .   .   .

YOU & ME

123 and we fall to the ground
Like children in the park
Digging in the sand
Like a castle on the beach
The waves tares it down
It's all just washed away.

And with this camera I'll paint a picture of you in the setting sun.

456 and we head toward the sky
Like an eagle diving down
Catching the fish in the river
Like an old tree in the wood's
The wind tares it down
It's all just blown away.

And with this high flying plane I'll take you from the rising moon.

And here we are standing in the night of the day, in the day of the night.

And as we go' the stars shine at us reflecting there glitter in the stormy sea.

& we're finally happy
& we're finally glad

789 and we run and crawl
Like the animal in the human
We have a craving feeling
Like the good & bad
The magic make's it all-right
It's all just forgotten in the end.

And with this love I'll keep you here on this planet called home.

& we're finally here
& we're finally together
- you & me -

RER'94 19/6

- JAILCITY'96 -

Providing confidential information
    & nearly all of us will be unemployed
        Before we can establish a new environment

            & then you speak to me in some unknown & foreign language
                Typical the words are way beyond reconition

Society appointed several lost hoodlums to find evidence
    To be in jail is an assasination of ones soul

        Dramatically you're more disinclined to be visible
           & there's an official limitation of confermation

        To be in jail results in a conclusionary
           Breakdown a Crackdown

        & needless to say that madness rules…………in <u>JAILCITY.</u>

RER'96 26/10 & 1/11

....But Can't....

I'm grounded

& there's nothing

I can do'

To change it

Coz' I'm scared

More then you

More then most

Raped in chain's of pain

& I look up in vain

& see behind a cloud of rain a plane

& it's flying away

& now it's gone

I want to feel, want to cry… but can't

I'm scared to try something new

Coz' I'm weak, fragile & don't think I can do it

I need someone to

Trust in me

& give me a chance, a helping hand

Before I slip away, into a crowed

Of forgotten soul's with

Lost dreams

& with a fading voice

I dissapear never to be found ever again, no ever again.

RER'96 13/11

- UFO - (so this is it) ?!… part. 3.

You don't know what's happened yet

& you lay there wondering
As I leave again in the blue -UFO-

I see you shriveled-up & blown away
Within a year, with a strange appearance on your face
& now you're free.

So it is this…no this is it.

- A REDWOOD FOREST -

Oh the saxophone
      Playing in the blue
           A blizzard engulfs it all
                & it's raining down with streamers
                    This disruptive excavation
                        Lift's me comparably higher
                            This critical evolution has no restrictions
                            Resources established with
                                  Excellence and enthusiasm

                                    In a redwood forest
                                    I see the tree's - are no more.

                            Application of membership increasing fast
                      Obtainment of information culminating quick
                Preservationists on parole
            Competitioners on patrol
        Distinctions in control

  As a redwood forest
I feel the intruders - cut some more

    The government do's one thing
        The cover-up of something
            The management say's one thing
                The statement gives another
                    With this increasing pain
                        & there's the coordinator?

                        In the redwood forest
                        I see the tree's falling - ones more

                                As additional versions appear
                          It's a risk in
                      Correcting the patterns
                  Of natures happenings
              In the redwood forest
            In the redwood forest
      I don't see the tree's anymore
The tree's aren't ever-more.

OCCASIONALLY REQUIERING MAINTENANCE

Over protectively & systematically
Selecting my choices

Subsequently & ineffectively
Restraining my motions

Non knowingly & mistakenly
Changing my appearance

And it's too late to do anything about it now
So meany fixations on non related things
That we're occasionally requiring maintenance
It's just genially unexplainable

Disturbingly & sensually
Stripping my soul

Gradually & successfully
Breaking my heart

Persistently & simply
Tearing me apart

ONGOING & ONCOMMING

My house is on fire
& I see pictures & other memories
    Burn away
        Burn away

I see a lake drying up
& I see the fish & other things
    Emerge
        Revealed

It feels like someone took my life
& squeezed it all out of me
It feels like someone took my life
& threw it in the trash

It's just a heroic failure to understand

There are meany unethical but necessary things to do'
When ones life just crumbles into dust as things do'

& I frequently try to get away
But it only happens in my head
Deep in my mind, deep in my mind, in my mind

I foresaw ongoing & oncoming dream's of truths

& in the end earthlings will have to build
Alternative accommodations for survival
For survival, for the future.

RER'96 27/10 & 2/11

EXSTRAVAGANT WALL OF FLAMES

Telling all I know
While'the sun is so close
That city's have melted

How can I keep running threw the mess of it all?

Should we rabuild it?
Or just leave it all to
Disintegrate.

Should we seek new and
Empty spaces to start all
Over again.

To start all over again, with this extravagant wll of flames

Now colliding with the sun
It's so hot that oceans have
Evaporated.

All mountains now turned to lava'
Can we keep on, or should we give up.

Now drowning in a inferno of flames
Burning in this heat
Liquefied in this extravagant wall of flames
In a ocean of pain

Everything seams so much clearer now.

I don't know if it's in being so pure or in being within this extravagant wall of flames
I'll burn like acid rain, in the fading shade, in the valley where tree's of ashes lay.

Now in one with the sun' shrinking to nothing and then explodes

And no-one realy cares coz' no-one's really around to see the spreading of us all

And this extravagant wall of flames are no more.

RER'95 &'96 6/2 & 30/3

FLOOD

& oh how the clouds over-come me.
    How they surround me & then it rains
        Down on me until it covers me
        & whatever I'm standing on.

            & it's only a flood
                Only a flood
                Only a flood

So now I'm under water & should be dead
But I'm breathing like normally
    It's just harder to get threw to the where
        One wants to go'

        It could be a thunderstorm a tidal wave,
            Tornado, a blizzard even
A volcanic eruption
        Or a avalanche, but it's only
            A flood

& now the moon is touching the surface
    Of my liquefied sky

        Can you feel the wind?
        Blowing by

But it was just a current.

COO COO!

I'm not a normal person
So why treat me so

It use to be easier to be me
Use to be easier to be at all

Standing staring into a room
In an apartment in the building
Across from
Across the street

Now hammering a nail into my head

Struggling to find a little peace
Franticly searching all my life
Swimming in your pool of lust
Enjoying every minute of it to.

I could see all of us lauging in the future somewhere
But couldn't see the things right in front of me here

It's depressing but true

I'm not a normal person
I'm weirder then most
Stranger theh you
Even a little coo coo co coo coo coo oooo o o o

I'm franticly desperately struggling?!… to escape my craziness.

10 stories up - part 1 of 3 out of 15 -

I know, like me you dream too

I know, like me you think your alone

But it's your life, it's your life

So please take control of it

        In-stead of living others
        In-stead og trying to be /
                        / somewhere else, someone else

        Concentrate about your self
          Do' what you want

                In-stead of doing what /
                            / other's do

I know, like em you feel so lost

I know, like me you don't know what to do /
                        / or where to go

        So be your self & take a chance
        Be your self & take a step.

RER'97 7/9

FROM THE SKY.....

In the city   I see it all decaying
                                              I see it all fall apart

In the city   I see it all pass me by
                                              I see it all com' to an end

In the city   I see everyone climbing to the top
                                                              Just to fall back down again

In the city   I see everyone trying so hard to make them selves
                                                                       Into someone, but for what?

In the city   I saw a little angel falling from the sky
                                                                    Something must have happened up there
                                                                       Is there war up in heaven now
                                                                             He crashed down like an
                                                                                       Airplane

Angel you use to be my little star shining in the sky

                     But where are you now, to show me the way
                     So where am I now, in the city?.

Part. 1.

- A beach bitch bench -

I see people runing franticly around
Trying to find a place
Trying to find there place… in life
Looking for a chair… to sit on
In front of a computer.
Searching thru the net
Seeking thru cyberspace
& then we go home
& eat a pile of pill's… for dinner
& so we go' to bed with a sheet of heat
& then we sleep
As we do so, someone's looking thru our dreams.

I see people running spasmodically around
Fighting thru crowds
Fighting thru clouds… of rain
WAR & PEACE, LOVE & HATE it's all the same.

As loud as you scream….I can't hear you
As big as you are……….I can't see you
As close as you might be I can't feel you
                      Can't be with you.

Coz' I hate your ways
& I'm waithing for the waves
To come crashing down / on a beach / as a bitch / on a bench, wait's
                                      Lifting weights
                                      Looking at tocxitwaste

There's a block out, no it's an outbreak
    There's an outtake, no it's a lockout

- But if it's ok for you / then it's all right by me -

RER'97 15,18 & 23/12

ANOTHER ORDINARY DAY

I didn't know
As I stand with my hands glued together
& my head in a mess
This couldn't be the end
& it's not the beginning

Oh another ordinary day
As another paranoid creature
Just another dysfunctional element

I can't do
What you ask me to'
As I stand here with my hands in a fix
& my life in a mess

In another ordinary day
In another protective way. . . I'm
Just another disrupted subject

I can't go'
Ias I stand here with my hands up in the air
& my hair in a mess
This could have been' the truth
But now it's all just one big lie

It's another ordinary day
Just another perfect morning
Just another destructive continuens

& in a unordinary way
It's all pratical & damageable
As we're all pretending & decaying

I didn't no
As I stand here with my hands teid together
It's like another pathological machine
But it's just another ordinary day. . . . .

RER'96 29 & 30/5

- MANIPULATION -
(?)

This is life & this is why
I feel so strange

All these games of war
All this wanting & waithing for things to happen

So if I do, what I want to
Then can I . . . . . be a part of life, & if anything at all, could I just be a part of your life?...

Sometimes I see clouds of pain coming over the land
& sometimes I see waves of rage crashing down on a beach
Sometimes I see destruction surrounding us
& sometimes I see flowers beneath us

But sometimes I see nothing at all
& sometimes I, like you just don't care.

RER'97 21/12

Out. Part. 1.

Out in the dessert
In the burning sun
In the meddle east
Feeling like melting butter

Out ine the forset
In the pouring rain
In the smug filled meadows
Breathing like never before

And the shade from the tree's
Enhances the veuw
And the glow from the moon
Enlightens my veuw

Then back out in a blizzard
In the twirling wind
In the frezzing cold

And all of everything we've ever try'd to manage
Just fall's apart, turns to stone.. . . & now I'm out of options
                                            Out of choices
                                            Out of questions
                                    Just out of portions

Then out in the sea
In the salty water
In a roaring tidal wave

And all of course
Because of man

And then in no-man's land I'm out of places to go'
                              Out of places to hide

And then the sudden gentle feeling of the wind softly blowing

And the sudden calm running of water flowing carefully on

And I'm just   out of things to dream about
                            Out of ways to get out!…

And I lay day after day in the same position as meany day's ago'

Sitting in a trance, in a kind of future-risdick past-tence

In the same place
In the same way
Trying not to say
That I can't stay

All these dreams
All these thoughts
All these ways to avoid it!?…

And still struggling to attempt to let out a verbal sentence
And still trying desperately to accept the rules of reality

Feeling left behind
Feeling so left out

Thow it's always been up to me, to get up - and get out.

THINK.

RER'98

THE END OF BOOK ONE.

Hope you like this book
And that the future book's will entrige
That you'll follow my evolution.

You can give your statement good or bad
Or a commet in between.

At: my book's   www.tropicalstormwritings.jimdo.com
                                        www.tropicalstormwritings.bodforfatter.dk

At: my travel's   www.miataiiix.dk

At: my music interests   www.myspace.com/claymenn

Or find me on Facebook.

COMMET PAGESE

SPECIAL THANX TO:

Mom & Dad for my life.

Sandy, Frederik, Jesper, Christian, Ian, Linda, Nicolas, Thomas for all the help.

All my friends and everybody else for witting pashently thru' the years
Listing to me say year after year I'm writing a book
And still nothing happened.

So this is for you guys.

and to all the band's that I've listen to between then and now thanx.

Robert E. Rose 20/10 2009

www.ingramcontent.com/pod-product-compliance
Lightning Source LLC
Chambersburg PA
CBHW081816220526
45470CB00007B/2336